Where Do BABIES Come From?

Sally Ann Wright and Honor Ayres

Pauline
BOOKS & MEDIA
Boston

Holly's mom was going to have a baby.
Her friend Ben's cat was about to have kittens.
Holly had been to the pond and seen
the baby ducklings. They were soft and fluffy.

Holly had been to the farm
and seen the baby piglets.
They had funny curly tails.

Holly went to the zoo and saw the baby elephant. He was sweet!

"Where do babies come from?" Holly asked her mom.

9

"All babies start with a mom and a dad," said Mom. "God made moms with tiny eggs inside their bodies. God made dads with tiny seeds. Together God made them able to make babies who grow inside the mom's body."

"When will our baby come out?" asked Holly.

"A baby elephant is inside its mother for nearly two years!" said Mom. "A baby zebra takes about twelve months. Our baby will have been inside me growing for about nine months.

"Our baby will be ready to be born in four weeks."

"But what does the baby do inside you all that time?" Holly asked.

"The baby moves and grows and eats and sleeps," said Mom. "The baby's heart, lungs, stomach, and brain are made. The nose, mouth, ears, and eyes are made, too.

"Our baby even has eyelashes and eyebrows. Our baby is a real, tiny person!

"Babies usually stay inside their mother's body until they are strong enough to be born safely."

"Why don't people all look the same?" asked Holly. "I don't look like Ben. Ben doesn't look like his big brother, Tom."

"God loves different colors and shapes and sizes," said Mom. "God made us all to look different and made us good at different things. You are special. No one else is quite like you. God knew you while you were growing inside me, and he loved you. He always will!"

"From the moment you were a tiny dot inside my body, God knew the color your hair and eyes would be. God knew what shape your nose would be and whether you would be tall or short."

19

"Will our baby look like me?" asked Holly.
   "You have a nose like mine and ears like
Daddy's. Your eyes are the same color as mine.
Babies all look something like their parents.
You and our new baby will look a bit alike."

"How will our baby come out?" asked Holly.
"Do the doctors have to make an opening
in your tummy?"

"Some babies do come out that way, but others push their way out of the mother's body through a special opening between her legs. Usually the mother understands when the time is right for that to happen, so she knows when to get ready."

"Will you still read me stories when our new baby comes?" asked Holly. "Will you have enough love for me, too?"

"I love you because you are you," said Mom. "I will love our new baby, too. You will be different from each other, but both very special. We will help each other and look after each other. That's why God put us in families—to love and help each other. And we'll all read lots of stories together!"

Wright, Sally Ann.

  Where do babies come from? / Sally Ann Wright and Honor Ayres. — 1st North American ed.

    p. cm.

  ISBN 0-8198-8311-5

1. Sex--Religious aspects--Christianity--Juvenile literature. 2. Pregnancy--Religious aspects--Christianity--Juvenile literature.
3. Sex instruction for children. I. Ayres, Honor. II. Title.

  BT708.W75 2007

  233'.5--dc22

2006014006

First edition, 2005

First North American Edition, 2007

Published by Pauline Books & Media, 50 Saint Paul's Avenue, Boston, MA 02130-3491. www.pauline.org

Printed and bound in Singapore

Pauline Books & Media is the publishing house of the Daughters of St. Paul, an international congregation of women religious serving the Church with the communications media.

1 2 3 4 5 6 7 8 9   14 13 12 11 10 09 08 07